→ KNOW

COWS

JACK BYARD

First published in Great Britain as *Know Your Cattle* in 2008 by Old Pond Publishing Ltd.
First published in North America in 2012 by Fox Chapel Publishing, 1970 Broad Street, East
Petersburg, PA 17520, USA. Published under license.

ISBN: 978-1-56523-613-4

Library of Congress Cataloging-in-Publication Data

Byard, Jack.

Know your cows / Jack Byard.

   p. cm.

ISBN 978-1-56523-613-4

1. Cattle. 2. Cattle breeds. 3. Cows. I. Title.

SF197.B996 2011

636.2--dc23
                                        2011017568

To learn more about the other great books from Fox Chapel Publishing, or to find a retailer near
you, call toll-free 800-457-9112 or visit us at *www.FoxChapelPublishing.com*.

Note to Authors: We are always looking for talented authors to write new books. Please send a
brief letter describing your idea to Acquisition Editor, 1970 Broad Street, East Petersburg, PA 17520

Printed in China
First printing

Contents

Acknowledgments

I am indebted to many cattle breeders and breed societies for their help in producing this book.

Picture Credits

(1) Kellythorpe Aberdeen Angus (2) Ayrshire Cattle Society, (3) Coyote Creek Farm, (4) Reid's Beefalo and Livestock, (5) Trey Sherer, (6) British Blue Belgian Cattle Society, (7) Temple Newsam Home Farm (Leeds City Council), (8) Gonsoulin Land and Cattle, New Iberia, LA, (9) British Bazadaise Cattle Society, (10) British Blonde Society, (11) Angela Hamilton, (12) CIMARRON Brown Swiss, (13) Patric Lyster, (14) The British Charolais Cattle Society, (15) Dale and Janice Price, Jandal Criollos, Winters, Texas, (16) The Devon Cattle Breeders Society, (17) Mark Bowles, (18) RE Archer Farms Ltd, (19) Helen McCann, (20) American Gelbvieh Association, (21) English Guernsey Cattle Society, (22) The Hereford Cattle Society, (23) Baylham House Farm, (24) Holstein UK, (25) National Milk Records, (26) The Kerry Cattle Society, (27) British Limousin Cattle Society, (28) Lincoln Red Cattle Society, (29) The Longhorn Cattle Society, (30) John Cameron, (31) (32) Murray Grey Beef Cattle Society, (33) The British Parthenais Cattle Society, (34) Craig Culley, (35) Wendy Robbins and Ian Stennett, (36) Callander Salers of Crieff, (37) Shetland Cattle Breeders Society, (38) Shorthorn Society, (39) British Simmental Cattle Society, (40) South Devon Herd Book Society, (41) The Sussex Cattle Society, (42) David Wynne-Finch, (43) www.rhuddelwelshblack.co.uk, (44) The Whitebred Shorthorn Society, (Aurochs) Porlock Visitor's Centre.

FOREWORD

Milk comes in cartons from the supermarket. Everybody knows that. When a group of children on a school trip were taken into a milking parlor they were amazed and shocked in equal proportions. Years of belief gone in a flash.

There are many different breeds of cattle, each with its own society or association working to promote cattle. I have tried with their help to give you a glimpse of the tremendous diversity.

Some have been here for a thousand years while others are just off the boat, mainly from Europe. The purity of the Jersey breed is jealously guarded, unlike that of the black and white Holstein cow and its Friesian cousin; their complex relationship would need Sherlock Holmes to unravel.

Some breeds are as rare as the Giant Panda, others are more numerous—but all need our protection. Many of the breeds in this book will become extinct if we do not support those small, local, or specialist producers who use them. Please support these producers by visiting your local supplier or farmers market. Use them or lose them.

Jack Byard

Bradford, 2010

COW TALK

There are a few words related to cattle, which to those not involved may seem like a foreign language. Here are just a few of these terms:

COW: Female cattle

BULL: Un-castrated male cattle

OX/BULLOCK: Castrated male cattle

HEIFER: A young cow

CALF: Baby cattle before weaning

BRINDLED: A colored pattern of spots or streaks

PIED: Patches of two different colors

ROAN: A dark coat with spots or hairs of grey or white

DUN: A grayish-brown color

HERD: The collective term for a group of cattle

POLLED: A cow born without horns

SWITCH: The tuft at the end of a tail

DRAFT ANIMAL: An animal used for drawing heavy loads such as a plow or cart

COMPOSITE BREED: A breed made up of two (or more) other breeds

Aurochs (Bos Primigenius)
The original ancestor of modern cattle

The Aurochs is the breed of cattle from which nearly all species of domestic cattle have descended and which became extinct in the British Isles about 3,500 years ago. According to records, it was black, stood 6 feet at the shoulder and had large curved horns, and existed in Europe, Asia and North Africa. The last Aurochs died in Poland of old age, according to Royal inspection records, in 1627.

AYRSHIRE

NATIVE TO
Scotland

NOW FOUND
North America and on most continents

World-quality milk ideal for yogurt, cheese and ice cream

The Ayrshire is any shade of red or brown with white. The patches are jagged at the edges and cover the entire body.

The improvement and development of the breed began in the mid-eighteenth century when the native breed was crossed with Teeswater and Channel Island cattle. During this period, it was known as the Dunlop and then the Cunningham before becoming the Ayrshire. By 1812, it was an established breed. For many years the elegant curving horns were the hallmark of the breed. The horns were 12 inches or more, curved upward, outward and backward, and were a magnificent sight when highly polished for the show ring. In modern farming, horns are impractical so today most Ayrshire cattle are dehorned as calves.

The Ayrshire is a strong, healthy, long-lived animal and an effective grazer. This makes it capable of surviving in less than ideal conditions such as the heat of Africa and the extreme cold of Scandinavia, while still producing world-quality milk that is ideal for making yogurt, cheese and ice cream.

BARZONA

NATIVE TO
Arizona, USA

NOW FOUND
USA

At home anywhere

The Barzona is mainly medium red but the color can vary from light to dark red. They can be with or without horns (polled).

In 1942, a Francis Norwood Bard and his wife, Phoebe, decided to develop a breed of cattle that could thrive on their ranch in the desert region of Yavapai County in Arizona. They wanted to produce a hardy breed that would graze naturally and produce more quality meat per head than the other breeds of the region. Four years later, Elliot S. (Jack) Humphrey joined Mr. Bard and took over the development and crossed the Africander, Hereford, Shorthorn and Angus breeds to create the Barzona. This sturdy animal is at home in the desert, the grasslands of the Midwest, the snows of the Northwest and the swamps of the Southeast.

In comparison to meat from their grain-fed counterparts, the meat from cattle that feed naturally on grass is ideal for the health conscious person. It is low in calories and is as high in Omega 3 as wild salmon, and has the same amount of fat as chicken.

BAZADAISE

NATIVE TO
Bazas, France

NOW FOUND
British Isles, Australia, Belgium,
Spain and Holland

Exceptionally tough
and vigorous

Bazadaise are light grey and slightly shaded in wheat color. The bulls are dark grey with a lighter saddle.

The Bazadaise (pronounced Baz-A-Day) originated in southwest France in the Middle Ages as a result of a cross between a local small grey cow called the Marini and a breed brought from Spain by the Moors. An exceptionally tough and vigorous animal, the Bazadaise will graze in the extreme cold of the high alpine meadows and the heat of the Spanish border region. The breed was once valuable as a working animal because it is able to work in extreme conditions ranging from the lowlands to the Pyrenees, a mountainous agricultural landscape on the border between France and Spain. Farm mechanization and war led to a decline in numbers. In France, the Bazadaise has achieved the coveted "Label Rouge," which is used to indicate produce of a superior quality.

Beefalo

NATIVE TO
USA

NOW FOUND
North America

Cross between domestic cattle and American bison

Beefalo are any cattle color and either horned or polled.

Beefalo are the result of crossing domestic cattle with the American bison.

Accidental crosses are documented as far back as the mid-eighteenth century when a passing herd of bison joined forces with a local cattle breed. It was in the mid-nineteenth century that Charles Goodnight, a former Texas Ranger, officially carried out a cross that he called a "Cattalo."

Goodnight and other like-minded breeders intended to create a hardy breed that could survive the harsh Kansas winters. Results were largely unsuccessful until the middle of the twentieth century when the mating of a domestic bull and a bison cow apparently produced the best results. This became the Beefalo. The Beefalo has the rare ability amongst cattle breeds to perspire, which means it can tolerate the heat as well as the cold.

Beefalo must have a maximum of 37.5% bison content; above that it becomes a Bison hybrid. The meat from Beefalo is low in fat and bad cholesterol and high in protein.

BEEFMASTER

NATIVE TO
Texas, USA

NOW FOUND
North America

Bred in Texas to resist heat,
drought and insects

Beefmaster are generally red and sometimes with mottled faces though there is no set color. They can have horns or be polled.

The Beefmaster is the first American composite breed and is a cross between the Brahman, Hereford and milking Shorthorn. The breeding program that led to the creation of the Beefmaster was started by Ed C. Lasater in 1908 and completed by his son, Tom Lasater, in the early 1930s. Having combined the existing crosses of Brahman/Hereford and Brahman/Shorthorn, Tom Lasater believed he had produced a superior animal. Tom Lasater's strict criteria were mainly fertility, weight, hardiness and milk with only the best of the best acceptable for the foundation herd.

Initially bred to survive in the difficult environment of south Texas, these excellent cattle are resistant to heat, drought and insects. They are gentle, intelligent and the females are excellent mothers. All of this and excellent beef—what more could you want?

The Beefmaster is the fourth most popular breed in the USA and was recognized by the U.S. Department of Agriculture in 1984 as a pure breed.

BELGIAN BLUE

NATIVE TO
British Isles

NOW FOUND
North America, Europe, Brazil
and New Zealand

Dual-purpose
meat-and-milk animals

The Belgian Blue mainly comes in white, black and blue roan, which is white hair over a base coat of a darker color. Red is seen occasionally.

The Belgian Blue, as you would expect, has its origins in central and upper Belgium. During the latter part of the 1800s, Shorthorn bulls were exported from the British Isles to Belgium to improve the local red and black pied cattle. The early twentieth century saw selective breeding to improve the quality of this dual-purpose meat-and-milk animal with the major breakthrough in 1960. The modern Belgian Blue was the result of this skillful breeding. The breed goes by many names the Moyenne et Haute Belgique, Belgian Blue-White, the Belgian White and Blue Pied and the Belgian White Blue. In America, the breed is often known as the American Belgian Blue; in Canada, it is the Canadian Belgian Blue; and in the UK, it is known simply as the British Blue.

BELTED GALLOWAY

....

NATIVE TO
Florida, USA

NOW FOUND
North America, the British, Australia, and Switzerland

Double coated, it thrives in cold and rainy climates

The Belted Galloway is black, red or dun colored with a white belt around its middle and is naturally polled.

The Belted Galloway's belted or "sheeted" appearance creates more questions than answers about its origins though it is without doubt an ancient breed. The Belted Galloway, often affectionately called "Belties," first appeared in Scotland during the 1500s, although references to sheeted cattle can be found as early as the eleventh century. The white belt is the only feature that separates the Galloway from the Belted Galloway. The characteristic was introduced by crossing the Galloway with the Dutch Lakenvelder.

Belties are double-coated, having a soft short undercoat with a long shaggy overcoat it sheds in hot weather. With about four thousand hairs per square inch, the double coat is a good raincoat and ideal insulation against heat loss. In addition, for the health-conscious consumer, the Belted Galloway has the same fat content as chicken and fish.

BLACK ANGUS ABERDEEN ANGUS

....

NATIVE TO
British Isles

NOW FOUND
North America and on most continents

America's most popular beef cattle

Angus cattle are predominantly black, but red does occur. They are polled.

The Aberdeen Angus originated in Aberdeenshire in northeast Scotland in the early nineteenth century. They are descended from the two local breeds of black cattle known as Hummlies and Doddies. Hugh Watson of Angus, Scotland, is considered the originator of the breed. He bought quality stock from near and far and used only the finest polled black animals for his breeding stock. In 1842, Old Jock, Watson's favorite bull, was born. Another star of the herd, a cow called Old Granny, was born in 1824 and is said to have lived for 35 years and given birth to 29 calves. Most of today's Black Angus can be traced back to those two animals.

The breed has a reputation for quality beef, established with the help of William McCombie, who was descended from a family of herdsmen. McCombie founded a herd based on Keillor stock and produced outstanding cattle he showed in England and France. Development and improvement have continued into the twenty-first century. Today, the Black Angus is the most popular beef breed in America.

BRAFORD

NATIVE TO
Florida

NOW FOUND
North and South America

Naturally bad-tempered, ideal for rodeos

Braford cattle are red with a white underbelly, head and feet. They can be horned or polled.

The breed was developed in Florida by Alto Adams, Jr. in 1947 by crossing Hereford and Brahman cattle with the intention of creating a breed capable of surviving extreme weather conditions. Initially it was not entirely successful. The first bulls had bad feet, eye problems and the Florida climate was not to their liking. Eventually calves were produced that were ideal breeding stock and they formed the Foundation Herd of the Braford.

The breed has amazing heat and insect resistance because of its Brahman ancestors. Their bulk, endurance and naturally ill-tempered disposition make them ideal for rodeos. It is believed a chemical in their blood responsible for their insect resistance also makes them bad tempered.

The Braford also produces quality, full-flavored meat. It is no longer considered a cross but is accepted as a breed in its own right.

BLONDE D'AQUITAINE

NATIVE TO
The Garonne Valley and Pyrenees mountains in the Aquitaine district of France

NOW FOUND
North America and most continents

Strong, hardy, lean and docile

Blonde d'Aquitaine is predominantly a wheat color but can range from almost white to brown.

Three strains of cattle have been used to develop the Blonde d'Aquitaine: the Garonnais, the Quercy and the Blonde de Pyrenées. The Blonde has been grazing the pastures of Europe since the sixth century and any breed that can survive for 1,500 years must have something going for it. They were originally used as draft animals and this continued until the end of World War II. Various crosses with the Charolais, the Shorthorn or the Limousin were attempted to improve the breed, known in Europe as the Blonde d'Aquitaine, but none were entirely successful and it was bred back to its original type. The breed was introduced to the USA in 1972.

The Blonde d'Aquitaine is strong, hardy, lean and docile and is renowned the low-fat quality of its lean meat that has led to its increase in popularity among health-conscious consumers.

BRITISH WHITE

NATIVE TO
British Isles

NOW FOUND
USA and Australia

A rare British breed that
survives in the USA

The polled British White is white with black or red points on its eyelids, ears, feet, nose and muzzle. They are polled.

The presence of the original British White in the British Isles can be traced back to the time of the Romans. When the Romans left, the cattle were left to roam wild. The modern British White is a direct descendant of these feral white cattle. It was the late-1800s before the cattle were domesticated again. The original herd began in Lancashire, England with a later herd being established in Norfolk.

In 1865, Rinderpest (or cattle plague), an infectious viral disease, arrived in the British Isles and 50,000 head of cattle had to be destroyed, leaving the British White at the point of extinction. The precautions taken at the time were the forerunner of those used 136 years later for foot and mouth disease.

The British White was imported sporadically into the USA before World War II, and in 1940, a small group was imported (allegedly on the instruction of Sir Winston Churchill). Today's British Whites descended from those foundation animals.

BROWN SWISS

....

NATIVE TO
Alpine region of Switzerland

NOW FOUND
North and South America, Europe, Australia, South Africa and New Zealand

Very popular dairy breed

The Brown Swiss varies from a very pale brown to almost chocolate colored with a creamy white muzzle, dark nose and dark blue eyes. When horned, the horns are short and white, growing darker toward the tips.

The Brown Swiss is the oldest of all dairy cattle. This handsome breed originated in northeast Switzerland, where skeletal remains similar to the Brown Swiss have been found in ancient lakeside settlements thought to date back to 4000 BC. Brown Swiss dairy cattle were developed from the Braunvieh dual-purpose cattle, the best milk producing Braunvieh having been chosen and selectively bred to create a quality milk-producing breed. Switzerland, the native home of the breed, has a reputation for producing quality cheeses.

In the summer months, the cattle are moved to the mountains to graze on the sweet pastures that are a product of the heavy spring rainfall. The Brown Swiss is the second largest dairy breed in the world with more than fourteen million animals.

CANADIENNE

NATIVE TO
Canada

NOW FOUND
In Canada

Docile small cow
unique to Canada

The calves of the Canadienne are light brown. As Canadienne age, their color turns to dark brown or black. They have a lighter color along the back and around the muzzle and udder. The skin is usually black pigmented.

The Canadienne, also known as the Black Canadienne, is the only dairy breed developed in Canada and is unique to the country. The breed was initially developed in France and selected for productivity and hardiness in the New World. Once imported, the Canadienne was improved through breeding with other imports from Brittany and Gascony in France.

In the 1850s, heavier cattle imported from Britain sidelined the breed. In 1895, a group of Canadians breeders who realized the breed was in danger of becoming extinct formed the French Canadian Cattle Breeders Association.

This docile, small animal takes full advantage of the early spring grass and is useful in the fall when heavier animals would cut up the fields. The Canadienne produces lean, quality meat and their superb milk is in great demand by cheese makers.

CHAROLAIS

NATIVE TO
Charolles, southeast France

NOW FOUND
In North America and most continents

Post-WWII newcomer to the USA

Charolais range from creamy white to tan with pink muzzles and pale hooves. There are also red or black varieties and they all have horns.

White cattle were grazing in the Charolles region in 878 AD and were known in the markets of Lyon and Villefranche. As with most continental cattle, the Charolais was a multi-purpose beast used as a draft animal, for milk and for food. It was bred for utility not beauty. It took the French Revolution to give the breed widespread popularity. In 1773, Claude Mathieu, a farmer in Charolles, moved with his white cattle to Nièvre in the region of Bourgogne where he improved the breed to such an extent that it became known, for a short while, as the Nivemas rather than the Charolais.

After the World War II, exports of the breed from France to other parts of the world began. Two bulls and ten heifers were imported into Mexico and six years later the breed entered the United States.

CRIOLLO

NATIVE TO
USA

NOW FOUND
North and South America

Of Spanish descent

Criollo come in any color except white, though many are black. They have a dense coat, hair in their ears and a heavy tail switch; the horns start horizontal and then curve forward and slightly upwards

Criollo (pronounced cree-o-yo) is a Spanish word describing something of Spanish descent born in the USA. Christopher Columbus brought the Criollo cattle's ancestors to the USA on his second voyage from 1493 to 1496.

These hardy cattle originated in the desert country of Andalusia and so developed the ability to cope with hostile conditions that would be too much for other breeds. This self-sufficient animal became popular across the western USA and northern Mexico where they are known as the Corriente.

In the nineteenth century, the beef industry became centered on the larger British and European breeds and the Criollo was pushed to the edge of extinction. Today the breed is fighting back. The steaks are smaller and leaner than those of heavier breeds and so ideal for the health-conscious consumer.

DEVON

NATIVE TO
England

NOW FOUND
USA, Europe, Australia and New Zealand

Came over with the Pilgrim
fathers in the 1620s

Devon cattle are red, with the color varying from a rich deep red to a lighter red.

The Devon is also called the North Devon to distinguish it from the South Devon, which is a very separate breed. Some authorities believe the Devon descended from two breeds of indigenous British cattle called the Longifrons and the Urus, as well as native Devon cattle. There is also evidence the Phoenicians brought red ancestral stock to British shores from North Africa or the Middle East on their frequent visits to buy tin. Could this be the reason the Devon is so adaptable to hot climates despite centuries of British weather?

In the 1620s, the Pilgrims took red cattle with them when they travelled to North America and the ship Charity delivered one bull and three heifers to the Plymouth Colony. They were the first purebred cattle to reach America.

DEXTER

NATIVE TO
Southwest Ireland

NOW FOUND
North America and on most continents

No bigger than a large dog

Predominantly black, but also red or dun, most Dexter cattle are horned but polled are becoming more readily available.

It is frequently heard that the Dexter is a comparatively new breed. In fact, it has been around for more than 300 years. A Mr. Dexter who settled in County Tipperary, Ireland, in 1750 developed this dual-purpose breed. They were carefully selected from the hardy mountain breeds descended from of the black cattle of the early Celts. The breed was further described in a report on Irish cattle in 1845 so is hardly a new kid on the block. The Dexter was introduced into the USA between 1905 and 1915.

This is a small, gentle animal, 36 inches to the top of its back (about the size of a St. Bernard dog) and a specialist at browsing low-quality vegetation. The Dexter produces quality meat that is much sought after. In the early twentieth century, they were the show cattle of the gentry, but by 1970, the Dexter was rare and endangered. Their popularity with small farmers fortunately caused a dramatic increase in their numbers and saved them from extinction.

FRIESIAN

NATIVE TO
Northern Holland and Friesland

NOW FOUND
Worldwide

Came to America
in the 1830s

Friesian cattle are predominantly black pied but red pied appear in small numbers.

The origins of the Friesian are unclear. Small black-and-white and red-and-white cattle were brought to Holland and Friesland from Jutland and crossing these with the existing Dutch cattle is believed to have created the basis of the modern Friesian. A preference for the black pied led to breeding in favor of this color, though the red pied still exists in small numbers in the Netherlands.

Friesians were imported into America around the 1830s. The Friesian is closely linked to the Holstein; in fact, it is difficult to tell them apart unless they stand together. The Friesian is today 75% Holstein though there is an increasing use of Friesian genetics because the benefits of the breed are being more appreciated today.

GALLOWAY

NATIVE TO
Southwest Scotland

NOW FOUND
North America, British Isles, Russia, South
Africa and Australia

Hardy breed thrives in
Scotland, Russia and Alaska

The polled Galloway is predominantly black, though the long outer coat may
have a chestnut tinge and small number of red can be seen.

The Galloway is one of the oldest and purest cattle breeds. Records show
that in the sixteenth century the native cattle of southwest Scotland
produced top-quality beef. The Galloway is an extremely hardy breed,
capable of living and calving in the harshest climates in places such as
Russia and Alaska. They are aided in tough environments by their double
coat, which is a soft downy undercoat and long oily overcoat. The Galloway
usually grazes wild upland countryside.

The Galloway is crossed with the Whitebred Shorthorn to produce the
Blue-Grey. In turn, the Blue-Grey female is crossed with European bulls
to produce excellent quality beef. In 2001, foot and mouth disease in
southwest Scotland and parts of England decimated the oldest and leading
herds of breeding stock. Only the dedication and hard work of the breeders
has returned the Galloway to the forefront of British cattle.

GELBVIEH

NATIVE TO
Bavaria in Southern Germany

NOW FOUND
USA and most continents

**Excellent mothers
of small calves**

The desired color of Gelbvieh cattle is a shade of yellow that one enthusiast describes as golden honey red, but black Gelbvieh are on the increase. They are usually polled.

The Gelbvieh (pronounced gelb-fee and translated as "yellow cattle") was developed in southern Germany at the turn of the eighteenth century and is one of the oldest German cattle breeds. The Gelbvieh was produced from local breeds in three districts of Bavaria to be used for food, milk and as a draft animal. Development continued into the late-nineteenth century. In the mid-twentieth century, red Danish cattle were introduced into the breed to improve milk production. The breed was imported into the British Isles in 1973 and has grown steadily in popularity.

Gelbvieh cows make excellent mothers and the calves are unusually small for such a large animal, resulting in fewer calving problems than similar European cattle. The Gelbvieh are noted for the quality of their milk.

GUERNSEY

. . . .

NATIVE TO
The island of Guernsey in the British Channel

NOW FOUND
North and South America, British Isles, Australasia and Africa

Lots and lots of
calcium-rich milk

There are many fanciful theories as to the beginnings of the Guernsey cow and the most common is unproven. In 960 AD, the Duke of Normandy sent a group of militant monks to defend the island of Guernsey against buccaneers and raiders, to cultivate the soil and educate the natives. They brought with them the finest French cattle, the Alderneys from the province of Isigny and the Froment du Léon from Brittany, with which they developed the Guernsey.

The Guernsey is renowned for the quality and the quantity of the milk it produces and its possible health benefits including protection against type 1 diabetes, autism and possibly heart disease. The milk is richer in calcium than any other and is also high in vitamin A and beta carotene, which gives the milk its rich color and is said to prevent a number of diseases including cystic fibrosis and arthritis.

HEREFORD

....

NATIVE TO
British Isles

NOW FOUND
Worldwide

Descended from the
cows of Roman Britain

The Hereford has a dark red coat and a number of distinguishing white markings including face, crest, brisket, legs and tail. There are two strains of Hereford: horned and polled.

The origins of the Hereford go back to times immemorial. Records in Herefordshire show the breed as early as the seventeenth century where it began as a draft ox, pulling plows, carts and sleds. The Hereford is descended from small red cattle of Roman Britain crossed with a large Welsh breed that grazed the border of Wales and England. It took its name from the county in which it evolved.

In 1742, Benjamin Tomkins produced, with two cows and a bull calf from his father's estate, what is accepted as the beginning of the true Hereford breed. The early breeders created the superb beef qualities that are still apparent in the breed today. Herefords are the first English cattle to be recognized as a true breed.

HIGHLAND

NATIVE TO
Scotland

NOW FOUND
North America and most continents

Vikings brought them to Scotland

The Highland can be black, red, yellow, brindle or dun.

The Highland breed has grazed and browsed the Scottish Highlands and western islands for more than 1,500 years and has played a major role in the area's development. There is speculation as to how they came to be there and the most likely suggestion is the Vikings took them there. The term for a group of cattle is herd unless you are of the Highland breed when the cattle are part of a fold. This term arose because the cowman would put his cattle into a fold at night to protect them from wolves and wild weather.

The Highland is double-coated with a soft downy undercoat and a long oily overcoat that can reach 6 inches. The outer coat protects against snow or rain and can be shed in hot weather. The long horns provide an excellent defense and the long forelock protects the eyes. For hundreds of years the Highland has provided food and drink for small farmers or crofters.

HOLSTEIN

NATIVE TO
North Holland and Friesland, Netherlands

NOW FOUND
Worldwide

America's milk cow -
President Taft kept one on
the White House lawn

The Holstein is easily recognized as a large stylish animal patterned in black and white.

The Holstein originated in Western Europe, particularly Holland and Friesland. The breed as we know it began in the mid-nineteenth century in the USA with the import of a bull and two calves from Holland by Vermont farmer the Hon. William Jarvis. There were other imports but unfortunately, these cattle were allowed to breed with local cattle so the Holstein breed was diluted and lost. Over the next few years further Holsteins where imported and these cattle formed the basis of the Holstein herd book. The Holstein and Friesian associations merged in 1885.

The average Holstein will produce approximately 2,370 gallons of milk a year. Pauline Wayne is possibly the most famous Holstein. She was the pet of President William Howard Taft and grazed the lawns of the White House, providing the president's household with milk. Today the Holstein is the most popular milk breed in the USA.

JERSEY

....

NATIVE TO
Jersey, the largest of the Channel Islands, 14 miles from the French coast

NOW FOUND
Throughout North America, British Isles, Australia, Denmark, New Zealand and Zimbabwe

Traveled to America
with the first colonists

Most Jersey cattle are shades of fawn and cream although darker shades are not uncommon. They always have a black nose with an almost white border.

There is only one breed of cattle on Jersey and to maintain the integrity of the breed, cattle imports have been banned for the past 150 years. The Jersey was once known as the Alderney and is descended from the Guernsey and the breeds found on the Normandy and Brittany coasts.

Records show the cattle were being officially exported in the 1700s, although before that time, emigrants from Jersey would take their cattle with them. The animals were welcomed aboard for the fresh milk they would provide on the voyage. On arrival at the American shore they were tossed overboard to swim ashore. Welcome to America. In Boston in 1638, Jersey-type cattle were sold for $39 each, a phenomenal amount.

Jersey milk is noted for its high quality rather than the quantity; it is high in protein, minerals and trace elements. Its rich natural color is derived from carotene extracted from grass.

KERRY

....

NATIVE TO
British Isles

NOW FOUND
North America and British Isles

Small and hardy, can survive
on sparse grazing

The Kerry is black with black-tipped white horns, though some are de-horned as calves.

The Kerry is descended from the Celtic Shorthorn, which was brought to Ireland by Mediterranean man and which still grazes the pastures of southwest Ireland today.

The Kerry is acknowledged as being one of the oldest breeds in Europe and the first breed developed primarily as a milk producer.

Records show Sanford Howard of Boston was possibly the first importer of the Kerry to these shores after a visit to Ireland in the mid-nineteenth century. To say Howard was impressed with the breed would be an understatement. He found it unbelievable that the small, hardy cattle lived at heights of up to 2,000 feet on poor quality grazing and still produced quantities of quality milk. The registered Kerry grazing today are descendants of cattle imported into Canada in 1970.

LIMOUSIN

NATIVE TO
The Central Massif between central and southwest France

NOW FOUND
North America and on most continents

Ancient cave paintings show
very similar cattle

The Limousin is mainly golden red, lighter under the stomach and around the eyes and muzzle. There are some black Limousin, which are born light fawn or brown and darken with age. Their black coats are tinged with brown. The Limousin can be either polled or horned. The horns are fine and point forward.

Cave paintings in the Lascaux Caves near Montignac, France, depict cattle very similar to the Limousin, which makes the breed an estimated 20,000 years old. The region in which the Limousin evolved is poor crop-growing country, so farming revolved around animals instead. The harsh, rainy conditions produced a sturdy, adaptable and healthy breed. Records show that in the seventeenth century, the Limousin was bred primarily as a draft animal and for food. In 1968, fifteen cattlemen founded the North American Limousin Foundation to develop and promote the breed. These beautiful golden cattle have now become and major part of the country's beef industry.

LINCOLN RED

NATIVE TO
England

NOW FOUND
North America and on most continents

Came to England with the Vikings

Lincoln Red are deep cherry red in color. They once had white, slightly incurving horns though the trend is now for the Lincoln Red to be polled.

Records of the Lincoln Red go back to the late-seventeenth century and DNA testing has proved it was introduced into the British Isles by Viking invaders between 449 and 600 AD.

In the late-eighteenth century, the local Lincolnshire breed was crossed with the Cherry Red Durham and the York Shorthorn, resulting in the Lincolnshire Red Shorthorn. In 1939, Eric Pentecost started the process of producing a breed without horns, and in 1960, the Lincolnshire Red Shorthorn became the Lincoln Red.

In the late-1970s, the breed's popularity suffered from the importation of European breeds so it was successfully crossed with selected European cattle to improve its commercial standing. This was done with extreme care to retain the Lincoln Red characteristics.

LUING

. . . .

NATIVE TO
The Scottish Isle of Luing

NOW FOUND
North and South American, Europe, New
Zealand and Australia

Sheds its heavy winter
coat in summer

Luing cattle are predominantly black pied but red pied in small numbers.

The Luing (pronounced Ling) originated on the Isle of Luing off the west coast of Scotland. The Luing is the result of skillful breeding by the Cadzow brothers in 1947 and was produced from the cross of a Shorthorn bull and a Shorthorn-cross-Highland heifer. The breed was developed through the economic need to produce a quality beef calf able to withstand the rigors of a harsh winter on the west coast of Scotland, where it had to survive high rainfall and poor quality grazing. The Luing has a heavy winter coat so does not need as much to eat to stay warm. The winter coat is shed in summer.

In 1965 the British Government recognized the Luing as a breed in its own right, and in the following years, it was exported to most continents. This strong, easily handled animal is exceptionally long-lived, usually living around 20 years. The Luing is a beautiful animal.

MEUSE RHINE ISSEL

NATIVE TO
Netherlands and Germany

NOW FOUND
North America, British Isles and Australia

Strong, docile and long-lived

The Meuse Rhine Issel is red and white.

The Meuse Rhine Issel, usually called the MRI, was developed in the Netherlands during the nineteenth century on the banks of three rivers from where the name originates: the Maas, the Rhine and the Ijssel. In Germany, the breed comes from the regions of Westfalia, Rhineland and Schleswig Holstein.

The German Breed Society was formed in 1900. Between 1920 and 1950, breeders in Denmark, Luxemburg, France and Belgium created their own red-and-white cattle using Dutch and German stock. Originally the MRI was bred as a dual-purpose animal for food and milk, although many farmers have quite recently gone entirely into milk production. The milk has the protein variant kappa casein-B, which is ideal for producing high-quality cheese and perfect for making ice cream.

The MRI, which was first imported into the British Isles in 1970, is strong, docile and long-lived. It has a high milk yield and produces top-quality meat.

KNOW YOUR COWS

MURRAY GREY

NATIVE TO
Upper Murray Valley, Australia

NOW FOUND
North America, British Isles, Australia and
New Zealand

A perfect 10 at the
Ohio State Fair

The Murray Grey has dark skin with a dark grey to light grey coat. It is polled.

The Murray Grey has progressed from an embarrassment to an international success. The first grey calves appeared by chance in a herd of black Aberdeen Angus cattle in the early twentieth century on the Sutherland farm in Thologolong on the New South Wales border. The docile grey cattle grew quickly and were efficient at turning grass into meat. Local farmers soon took notice of their qualities and began developing the breed. By the mid-twentieth century, the Murray Grey was a commercial success and the Murray Grey Beef Cattle Society was formed. The growth of the breed in Australia was unprecedented and its high-quality meat was of the type that was in great demand in Japan and Korea.

The Murray Grey was first imported into North America in the 1970s and has gone from strength to strength, winning major competitions at the Calgary Stampede and at the Ohio State Fair, where it was awarded a perfect 10 for quality.

PARTHENAIS

NATIVE TO
Parthenay Region, France

NOW FOUND
USA and British Isles

High quality low cholesterol meat

From light tan to ginger-red with soft dark eyes and a black nose, hooves and ear tips. They are naturally horned but dehorned soon after birth.

The Parthenais (pronounced Par-Te-Na) is one of the oldest breeds in France and the herd book dates back to 1893. Until the 1950s the Parthenais was used as a draft animal for pulling plows and carts, after which it became a beef breed also used for milk. It is a strong, adaptable animal with the ability to survive in extreme climates and all farming systems from intensive to ranch grazing.

The calves are dehorned shortly after birth to avoid damaging each other as they grow. The Parthenais was introduced into the USA in 1990 and can now be found in many areas of the country. For the health conscious, the Parthenais produces quality low-cholesterol lean meat.

PIEDMONTESE

NATIVE TO
Piedmonte Region, Northwest Italy

NOW FOUND
USA, British Isles and Europe

Calm and friendly,
which farmers like

The Piedmontese is white or light grey. Newly born calves are golden brown but within months take on their adult color. Older bulls become dark grey with darker patches on the head and neck.

Archaeological findings, fossil remains and rock paintings trace the breed's ancestors back to the Aurochs type. The Aurochs lived a minimum of 10,000 years ago, which makes the Piedmontese a truly ancient breed.

About 25,000-30,000 years ago another breed, the Zebu, migrated from what is now western Pakistan, reaching, but not crossing, the Alps. The Piedmontese derives from the interbreeding of the Aurochs and Zebu. "Piedmonte" translates as "at the foot of the mountain," in this case, the Alps. The breed is calm and friendly, a very desirable trait for farmers. For the health conscious, the meat has exceedingly low cholesterol content.

RED POLL

NATIVE TO
England

NOW FOUND
USA, British Isles, Australia and New Zealand

Hardy, long-lived
and economical

The Red Poll is dark red or rich brown with no white markings apart from the switch or tuft of the tail. It is naturally polled.

The Red Poll is the result of crossing two ancient, and now extinct, breeds, the Norfolk Red and the Suffolk Dun. James Reeve, a tenant farmer, did this in the early nineteenth century. The Norfolk was the horned beef breed and the Suffolk a polled dairy breed with a history dating back to the Roman occupation of Britain. The result of the cross was a naturally polled dual-purpose breed producing milk and beef of superb quality. The Red Poll Cattle Society was formed in 1888.

The Red Poll is a hardy, long-lived and economical breed that does not require large amounts of food to remain healthy. In the mid twentieth century, Red Poll numbers went into a serious decline and it was classified as rare. The dedication of the breeders and the quality of the Red Poll has reversed this trend and the breed is once more taking its rightful place in commercial farming. The year 2008 was the 200th anniversary of the breed.

SALERS

NATIVE TO
Cantel Region, Southcentral France

NOW FOUND
USA and British Isles

Browsing and grazing in
France for 7,000 years

Salers are mainly dark red mahogany but there is an increasing number of black. They can either be horned or polled.

The Salers (pronounced Sa-lair) is one of the oldest breeds in the world, and has been grazing in France for more than 7,000 years. Cave paintings near the small medieval town of Salers depict the breed, which is very similar in appearance to ancient Egyptian cattle.

The Salers was first imported into the USA in the 1970s, making it one of the last breeds to be imported into North America. American cattlemen were looking for a breed to improve their livestock and the Salers were the answer. Their native homeland has poor soil and a harsh climate and so the breed has developed to produce milk and beef despite difficult conditions.

The region in which the Salers were bred was isolated and free of other cattle breeds and so it is said to be one of the most genetically pure of all European breeds.

SALERS

SHETLAND

NATIVE TO
Shetland Islands

NOW FOUND
British Isles

Eats seaweed and dried fish
when there's no grass

Shetland cattle are predominantly black and white, but red and white occurs. They have short horns similar to those you would expect to see on a Viking's helmet.

The Shetland is a truly ancient breed with remains having been found in archaeological digs dating back to the Bronze Age. It is thought to be a descendant of the ancient and dangerous wild cattle, the Aurochs.

The Shetland was traditionally a house or crofter's cow and would supply a family with food and drink. The Shetland is a calm animal and easy to handle. It is a hardy animal able to survive on poor-quality fodder—when the grass is gone the Shetland can eat seaweed and dried herring. For the crofter, this was an important characteristic because the death of a cow would have been a tragedy perhaps leading to starvation.

The modern Shetland is ideal for the small farmer because its lightweight frame makes it less likely to churn up good pasture in wet weather. For the health conscious, Shetland milk has good levels of unsaturated fatty acids and low levels of saturated fatty acids.

SHORTHORN

NATIVE TO
England

NOW FOUND
North America and on most continents

Red-and-white coloring is unique

The Shorthorn is red, red-and-white or white-and-roan. This particular roan color is a mixture of red and white and is found in no other cattle breed. Shorthorns can be horned or polled.

The Shorthorn has evolved over 200 years from the Durham and Teeswater cattle of northeast England. In the late-1700s, the brothers Charles and Robert Colling improved these two breeds using techniques Robert Bakewell had developed years earlier to improve the Longhorn cattle. In 1783, Charles Colling acquired four cows named Duchess, Cherry, Strawberry and Old Favourite, and at this time became aware of superior calves at a local market. The calves were bred from a bull called Hubback, which Colling bought for $12. This shrewd move led to the birth of a bull named Comet in 1804, which Colling sold six years later for $1,600.

In the early twentieth century, the Shorthorn was a dual-purpose breed, but specialization for milk and beef led to the breeders starting separate societies for milk and beef herds.

SIMMENTAL

NATIVE TO
Switzerland

NOW FOUND
North America and on most continents

Docile, adaptable and happy on a small farm

Color varies from gold to red, which may be evenly distributed in defined patches on a white background. The head is white and sometimes there is a white band across the shoulders. They can be polled or with upturned horns.

The Simmental originated in the Simmen Valley in the Bernese Oberland. It is now the most numerous breed in Europe and among the most numerous breeds in the world, exceeded only by the Brahman. The Simmental is a cross between a small Swiss native breed and a large German breed and has a history dating back to the Middle Ages. The breed was being exported to Italy as early as the fifteenth century and to most of Eastern Europe, the Balkans and Russia in the nineteenth. By 1895 it had reached South Africa.

The Simmental is a docile, adaptable animal and is as happy on a rural small farm as it is in a more commercial farming operation.

South Devon

NATIVE TO
England

NOW FOUND
USA, British Isles, Australia and New Zealand

The largest British cow came to America on the Mayflower

South Devon cattle are a rich medium-red with copper tints, which can vary in shade. Most South Devons have horns but polled animals do exist.

The South Devon, the largest of British native cattle, has grazed in the southwest of England for more than 400 years and is thought to have descended from the red cattle imported by Norman invaders in 1066. Because of their size and docile nature, the breed is known as The Gentle Giant.

In 1620, the South Devon's predecessors were taken aboard the Mayflower from Plymouth to the North American colonies. They were later used to supply staple food to the Royal Navy. Until well into the 1800s, this powerful animal had been relied upon to pull the plow, as well as to supply food and drink. In the nineteenth and twentieth centuries careful selective breeding took place to further improve the breed.

KNOW YOUR COWS

SUSSEX

NATIVE TO
England

NOW FOUND
USA, Australia and South Africa

Amazing tolerance
for heat and cold

The Sussex has a smooth dark red coat with white tail switches.

The Sussex is a truly ancient breed probably originating from the horned red cattle that grazed the dense forests of the Weald in Sussex and Kent around the time of the Norman Conquest. The earliest mention of a purebred Sussex was in 1793.

The Sussex was once noted for producing strong, powerful oxen ideal for working the heavy land, so was used as a draft animal until this work was taken over by horses and tractors. The Sussex was then bred for food.

The Sussex is a placid, adaptable animal with an amazing tolerance to heat and in the winter it grows a thick curly coat enabling it to survive the coldest Sussex conditions. It is also an efficient forager, able to survive and remain healthy on poor-quality grazing.

TEXAS LONGHORN

NATIVE TO
Texas, USA

NOW FOUND
North America

Cattle that won the West

Texas Longhorns can be just about any color. Usually, a cow can produce a calf that may look entirely different than either parent.

The Texas Longhorn could be called the cattle that won the west. They arrived in America with the Spaniards, via the Moors, who had brought these long-horned cattle from Africa. Many of these beautiful, hardy, disease-resistant cattle escaped from the basic corrals built by the Spanish or were abandoned after ranch failures. They scattered to live in the harsh wilderness.

Three hundred years later, Civil War soldiers returning home rounded up three million wild Texas Longhorns and shipped them to the voracious market in the east.

In the 1870s and 1880s, the Texas Longhorn was nearly driven to extinction, but it was prevented thanks to a few families and a government refuge. They are now being bred to improve their horn, color and conformation. Their meat is ideal for the health-conscious consumer because it is lower in cholesterol, fat and calories than other breeds.

WAGYU

NATIVE TO
Japan

NOW FOUND
USA, Europe and Australia

Low cholesterol meat

Wagyu are black or red though black is the dominant color.

'Gyu' is the Japanese word for cattle and the term 'Wagyu' covers four main breeds. The Wagyu is considered the caviar of beef. In 1976, several animals were exported to the USA for research into improving American cattle with their superior genetic qualities. Before then, the export and breeding of Wagyu cattle outside Japan was forbidden.

Originally, the majority of the Japanese population was Buddhist and therefore vegetarian, so the Wagyu was a draft animal used in the production of rice. However, the Shoguns who ruled Japan from the late-twelfth century to the late-nineteenth century found their warriors became stronger if they ate meat.

The Wagyu were given only the best grain to eat and beer to drink and were massaged three times daily. The latest research from Pennsylvania State University shows that eating Wagyu beef can reduce cholesterol.

WELSH BLACK

NATIVE TO
Wales

NOW FOUND
North America and on most continents

Among the world's oldest and purest breeds

Welsh Black cattle vary from jet black to rusty black, but occasionally are red. They can be horned or polled.

This native British breed has existed in the Welsh hills and mountains since long before the Roman invasion. It is a possible descendant of cattle from the Iberian Peninsula. The modern-day Welsh Black is the result of 90 years of selectively breeding two Welsh breeds: the North Wales type, raised in the hilly and mountainous regions, and the South Wales type, from a lower and gentler landscape. The Welsh Black is possibly one of the oldest and purest breeds in the world.

The breed is hardy and adaptable, growing a thick coat in winter, which enables it to graze in snow and rain when most other breeds would head for cover. It is happy grazing in the lowland areas or foraging in the uplands. This adaptability enables the Welsh Black to survive when many other breeds would starve.

WHITE PARK

NATIVE TO
British Isles

NOW FOUND
USA, Germany, Denmark, Australia
and Canada

King James named it 'Sir Loin'

White Park cattle are large and white with black points on the ears, muzzle, eye rims and feet. They have elegant, wide-spreading black-tipped horns.

The White Park is a rare and ancient breed that has been browsing and grazing in the British Isles for more than 2,000 years. Don't confuse the White Park with the British White or the American White because, though they share color and looks, the White Park is genetically an entirely separate breed. The nearest relatives to the White Park are in fact the Highland and Galloway cattle of Scotland. During the Middle Ages, the landed gentry kept herds in enclosed parks, but as fashions changed in the late-1800s, the numbers dwindled. The White Park was heading toward extinction. In 1941, under threat of German invasion, five cows and one bull were dispatched to Pennsylvania, reputedly on the orders of Winston Churchill. Later additions were the beginnings of the White Park cattle in America.

The White Park could possibly be the source of the word sirloin coined by King James I. It is sometimes claimed he enjoyed his White Park steak so much that he knighted it and so ate, the very first "Sir Loin."

More KNOW YOUR ANIMALS Books

Know Your Chickens
By Jack Byard

Forty-four breeds of chicken—some rare, each with a rich diversity of color, size and feather pattern.

ISBN: 978-1-56523-612-7
$6.95 • 96 Pages

Know Your Pigs
By Jack Byard

Twenty-eight breeds of pigs—from the American Guinea Hog to the Wild Boar.

ISBN: 978-1-56523-611-0
$6.95 • 64 Pages

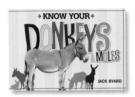

Know Your Donkeys & Mules
By Jack Byard

Thirty-five breeds of donkey—from miniature to the mammoth with a co of mules thrown in.

ISBN: 978-1-56523-614-1
$6.95 • 80 Pages

Look For These Books at Your Local Bookstore or Specialty Retailer
To order direct, call **800-457-9112** or visit *www.FoxChapelPublishing.com*

By mail, please send check or money order to:
Fox Chapel Publishing, 1970 Broad Street, East Petersburg, PA 17520

# Item	Shipping Rate	
1 Item	$3.99 US	$8.98 (
Each Additional	.99 US	$3.99 (

International Orders - please email info@foxchapelpublishing.co
or visit our website for actual shipping costs.